Off-Road Recovery Techniques

To
Nicola and Sue
whose patience was appreciated.

Can I help?…

Off-Road Recovery Techniques

A Practical Handbook on Principles and Use of Equipment

Nick Cole

Motor Racing Publications Ltd

MOTOR RACING PUBLICATIONS LTD
Unit 6, The Pilton Estate, 46 Pitlake, Croydon CR0 3RY, England

First published 1996

Copyright © 1996 Nick Cole and Motor Racing Publications Ltd

All rights reserved. No part of this publication may be reproduced, stored in a retrieval system, or transmitted, in any form or by any means, electronic, mechanical, photocopying, recording or otherwise, without the prior permission of Motor Racing Publications Ltd

British Library Cataloguing in Publication Data

Cole, Nick
    Off-road recovery techniques: a practical handbook
        on principles and use of equipment
    1. Automobiles – Off road operation
    I. Title
    629.2'83042

ISBN 189987013X

Disclaimer of Liability
The information in this book is true and complete to the best of our knowledge. All recommendations are made without any guarantee on the part of the author or publisher, who also disclaim any liability incurred in connection with the use of this data or specifications.
    We recognize that some words, model names and designations, for example, mentioned herein are the property of the trademark holder. We use them for identification only. This is not an official publication.

Printed in Great Britain by The Amadeus Press Ltd, Huddersfield

CONTENTS

INTRODUCTION	7
PICKETS, HOLDFAST and DEADMAN ANCHORS	11
Pickets	11
Holdfast anchors	14
Deadman anchors	16
WINCHING	19
BRIDGING	27
TRACTION AIDS	33
Traction	35
LIFTING	37
TOWING	41
TESTING AND INSPECTION	43
GENERAL	47
APPENDIX A – ROPES	51
APPENDIX B – FRICTION	53
APPENDIX C – BRIDGING DATA	56
APPENDIX D – ELECTRIC WINCH DATA	61
APPENDIX E – CONVERSION FACTORS & FORMULAE	63
APPENDIX F – TYPICAL VEHICLE WEIGHTS & CAPACITIES	69
REFERENCES	70
REGISTERED TRADE MARKS AND PHOTOGRAPHIC CREDITS	71

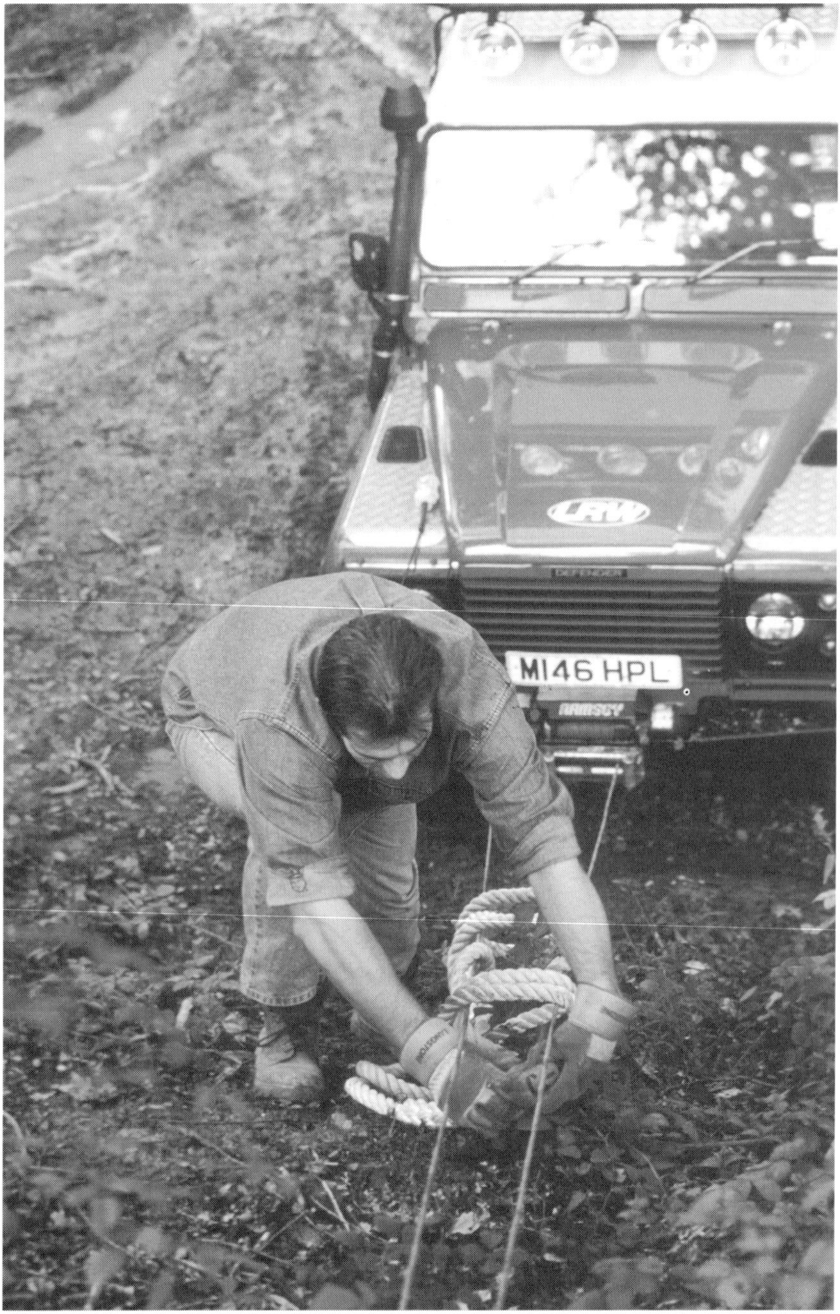
LRW
M146 HPL

INTRODUCTION

Self and assisted recovery is largely a matter of common sense. However, it needs to be based on experience and careful thought. It is far too easy to make a difficult situation worse and apart from the need to be extricated, safety has to be a prime consideration. This manual discusses the employment of various pieces of equipment, together with some principles and guidelines about effective use of natural materials, all accompanied by tables, charts and other data.

The data in this handbook implies an element of precision which is not strictly true. Because of the variability of vehicles, equipment and ground condition, it must be up to the operator to ensure that he or she errs on the side of caution and attempts an alternative before disaster occurs or is made irrecoverably worse. There are too many variables for recovery to be an exact science, but providing the principles are understood and care is taken a casualty can be safely and successfully recovered.

Safety factors are used to ensure working loads on structures and materials are well below the elastic limit, beyond which failure occurs. For lifting purposes a factor of 4 is used and is a helpful guide. When towing or pulling it is the norm to work with much less stringent limits, particularly when using lightweight portable equipment. Normal safety factors result in greatly increased weight, with structures or components being highly derated and hence 'over-engineered'. However, using equipment at levels higher than the normal safety limits could involve claims of negligence from the Health & Safety authorities in the event of an incident.

This manual is the culmination of research based on experience and a compilation of other published engineering data from a variety of sources. Of course, in the field it may not be possible to find a convenient tree, log, boulder or whatever and the ground may well be less stable or have a camber. In these circumstances safety factors may have to be ignored or reduced. Unfortunately, it is therefore not possible for the author to accept any liability for any disasters that may ensue. Common sense should always prevail, and time taken to watch what is happening while doing it can prevent a situation

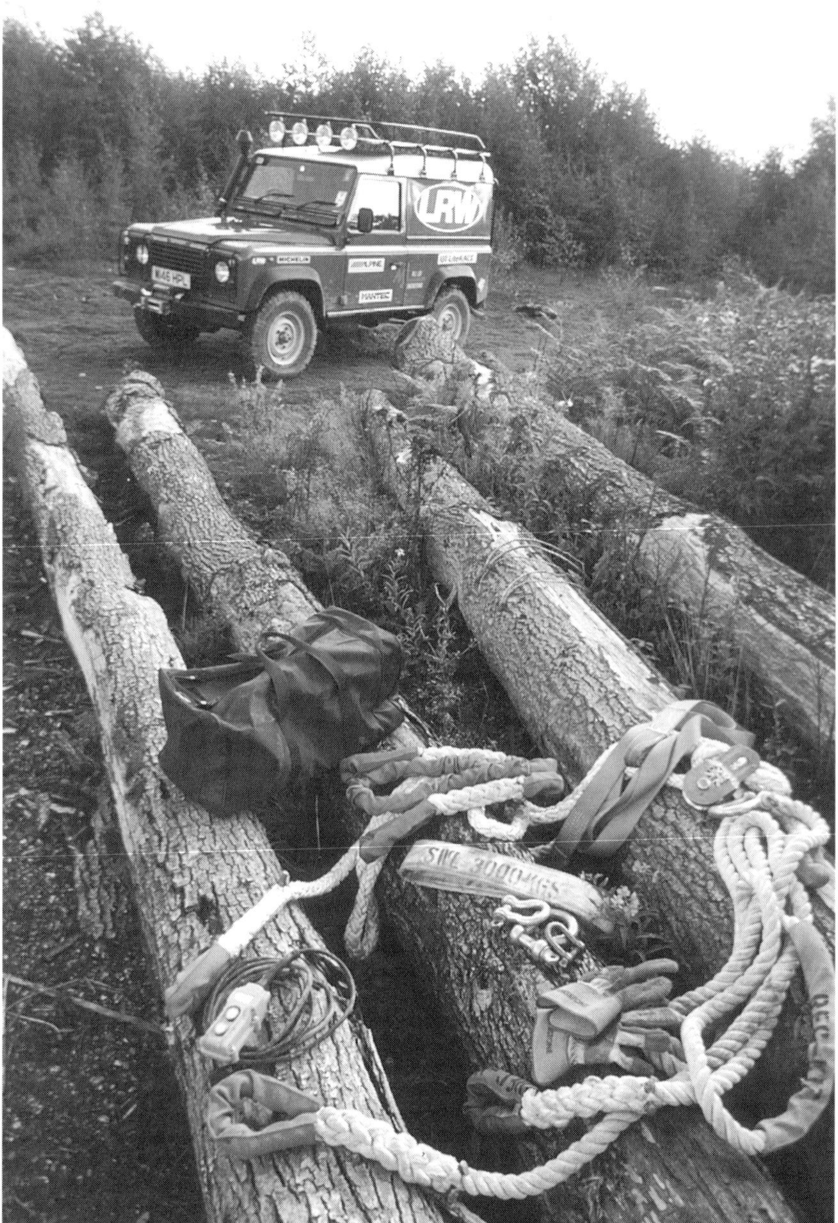
LRW
SWL 3000KGS

being made worse. No matter how undesirable it is to admit defeat it may be better to walk out and seek additional help.

Just as with crossing unknown terrain for the first time, the golden rule is to stop, look and plan a course of action. An experienced operator will be able to judge by eye what is or isn't suitable. For those who do not have a great deal of experience or wish to review previous skills, this handbook will provide a convenient *aide-memoire*.

The measurement units used in this manual are usually SI, ie kilograms and metres. However, the exceptions occur when areas are being discussed. Here, a hybrid unit kg/ft^2 is used. This is for estimating purposes as square feet are easier to judge than square metres, $200kg/ft^2$ being easier to guess than $2,153kg/m^2$, for example. For further simplicity, mass units kg are used whenever pulling loads are discussed, when strictly speaking force units kgf should be used. For virtually all practical earth-bound purposes there is no distinction between mass in kg and pulling force in kgf. The intention in this manual is to provide a ready reckoner for field use where the luxury of exact science and measurements are not possible. The author apologizes for any confusion, but where used the units should be obvious.

Comments, suggestions or error corrections will be welcomed by the author.

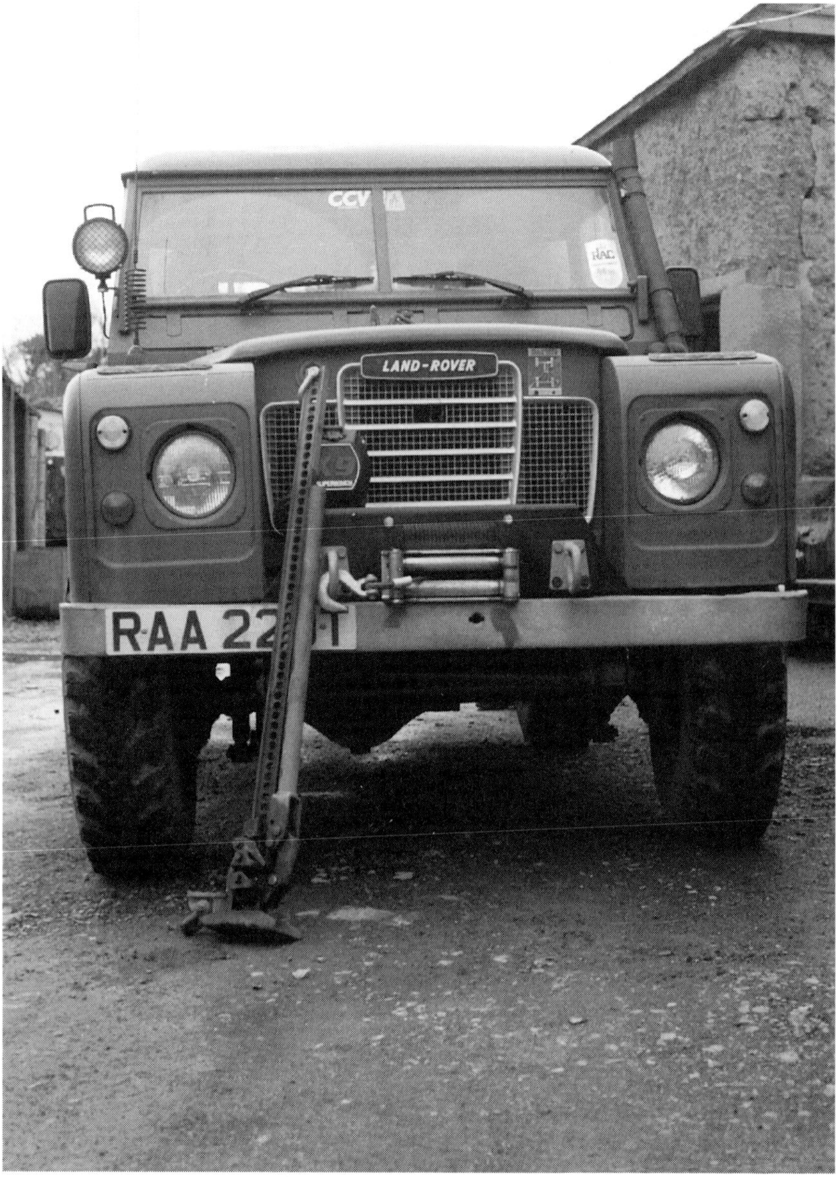
LAND-ROVER
RAA 22

PICKETS, HOLDFAST AND DEADMAN ANCHORS

PICKETS

A picket is a stake driven into the ground for the purpose of anchoring a device or rope. The effectiveness is entirely dependent on the nature of the ground and in general the effect of topsoil can be ignored. Any readily transportable picket will provide most of its holding power in the lower section and will tend to bend between the surface and 12in to 24in down. Providing the load does not snatch and the subsoil is in firm condition, even when bent a good broad picket will often stay in the ground. The only effective way of holding against topsoil is to increase the bearing area by several orders of magnitude, which is not a practical option for simple transportable devices.

Considerations when using any anchor are the pulling angle and amount of material between the anchor and casualty. The lower the angle and the greater the depth of the bearing area the higher the holding power. Any anchor needs to be well over 12in below the ground to be effective. The nature of the ground is crucial: a well compacted and solid material will require less bearing area whereas soft, wet or sandy ground will require significantly more for the same holding power.

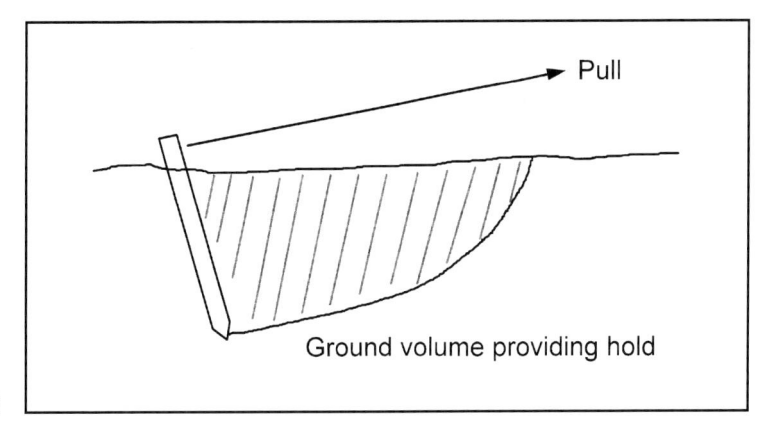

Figure 1

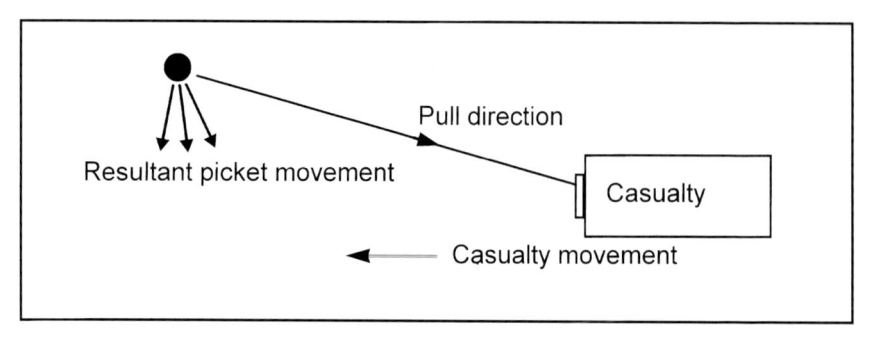

Figure 2

Unless a picket or anchor is set exactly in line with the pull it will tend to collapse sideways. This collapsing movement will cause a rotation about the picket depending on the relative positions which change as the casualty is moved along. 'T'-section pickets are particularly vulnerable as they are strongest directly in line with the central web. Any sideways pull will bend them more easily than angle section used in the same position.

A picket will tend to bend at some point below ground level. This is caused by the topsoil shifting and not providing a solid purchase for the picket to hold against. As the holding power is dependant on the depth, there is a significant bending moment along the length of the picket. This bending force increases from the bottom of the picket and is greatest at ground level. Unfortunately, at shallow depths the holding power is very low and the soil tends to be 'bulldozed' in the direction of the casualty and the loss of bearing surface causes the shaft to bend. Some devices are available that increase bearing area, but they only operate in the topsoil and are not generally any more effective than a plain picket. They are usually constructed with some sort of linkage to a blade or similar wide plate. The risk of collapse with these is very high especially if not exactly in line with the pulling direction. As these enhancements only operate in the topsoil it can be seen from Chart 1 that they will not provide any significant additional holding power for all the complication and bulk. One square foot of bearing area at 1 foot depth will hold against about 100kg, at 3 feet about 1400kg, and at 6 feet about 3,100kg, whereas a 3ft picket on its own fully set in the ground holds up to 310kg. Getting 1 square foot of bearing area 3 feet down is an arduous task! Experiments with winged and plain pickets for a given pull produced the same amount of bending, yet both stayed in the ground. Self-setting 'anchors' are large, unwieldy and so specialist that they are unlikely to have a useful secondary function, and wide-winged pickets are very difficult to set at any useful depth. The extra expense, weight and handling difficulty is pointless unless the ground conditions justify their use. Simple multi-role devices are more effective, lighter and can invariably be used or adapted for

Picket ground anchor, to hold around 1200kg of pull depending on the ground.

other purposes. This is an important consideration when reviewing weight/ effectiveness ratios and planning what equipment should be carried.

Many things can be used to make a picket: sharpened wooden stakes, steel angle, tubing and so on. The physical properties of natural materials can be limited and if you are relying on finding something useful lying around you are liable to be disappointed. Invariably there will be nothing suitable to hand or it is just out of reach of all your ropes! To be safe, carry ready-made pickets. A good one will be capable of being driven into the ground several times, will

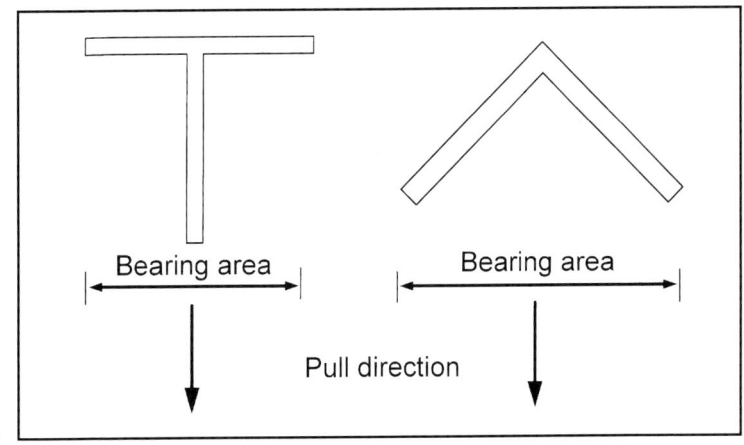

Figure 3

13

have lifting handles to assist with removal and some means of attaching or locating ropes and chains.

Steel pickets are usually made of 'T' or angle section. 'T'-section is more resistant to bending in line with the central strut but has 30% less bearing area, size for size than angle. Since it is the bearing area that is of most importance when holding a pull, unless the picket bends enough to pull from the ground no advantage is gained with 'T'-section. The 'T' picket must be set and maintained exactly in line with the pulling direction to utilize the greater strength. Any misalignment will mean it is no better than conventional angle section and will be less resistant to bending than angle which is stronger off-centre. Ropes or chains should be attached no higher than ground level otherwise the extra leverage will more easily bend the picket and possibly pull it from the ground. The forces actually required to pull a picket from reasonably firm subsoil are quite high, and even if bent a picket will often hold the load. Rod or pin types of pickets are very useful in hard ground as they are easy to set, but are very prone to bending; a large number are required to sustain any reasonable load.

HOLDFAST ANCHORS
A holdfast is a combination of pickets lashed or linked together to increase the area bearing against the ground. Multiple pickets lashed together and driven into the ground as a single unit increase the surface area and also the effective resistance to bending.

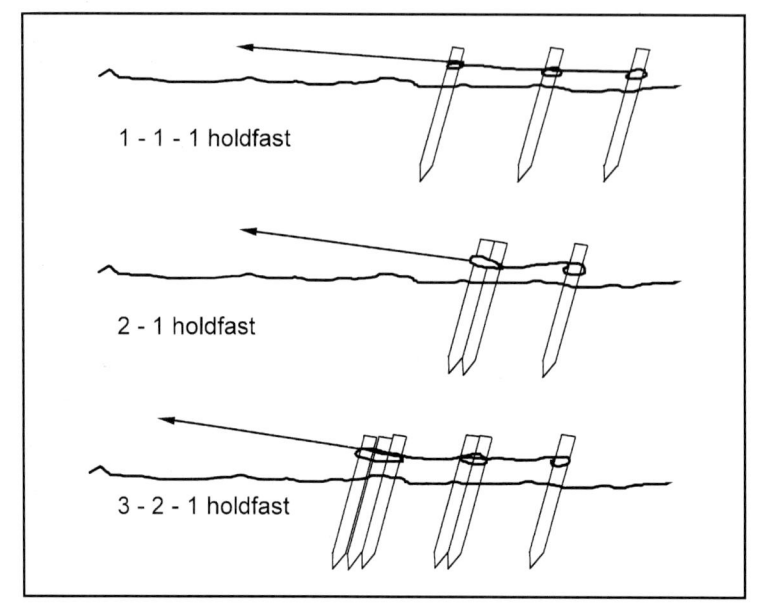

Figure 4

Pickets driven 1m into the ground, spaced 1 to 2 metres apart, inclined away from the load at about 15° should hold a pull as shown in Table 1:

Type	Undisturbed earth (kg)	Wet clay and gravel (kg)	Wet river clay and gravel (kg)
Single	310	280	150
1 – 1 holdfast	630	570	310
1 – 1 – 1 holdfast	810	730	400
2 – 1 holdfast	900	810	450
3 – 2 – 1 holdfast	1810	1630	900

Table 1

Pickets can be joined by ropes, chains or rigid frame assemblies. Flexible lashings lead to picket movement and loosening in the ground as ropes tend to stretch or give at the knots and chains are inherently loose unless tightened with tensioners. Twisting a bar in the lashings helps, but can be difficult to achieve as the bar will be obstructed by the ground. Frame or plate assemblies are the preferred option. These are used by the military and several proprietary styles are available commercially. Military holdfasts use a very heavy curved plate and are designed to take hi-tensile steel pins. They spread the load across the pins but require many of them as they offer a very small bearing area. Frame assemblies can be constructed to take a number of pickets. If dimensioned carefully they will tend to lock with any picket movement and provide an increased load capacity and resistance to bending when compared with ropes or chains. Using frames and pins avoids the need to carry complicated assemblies and thus can be put to alternative uses as

A 1–1 holdfast, using rope to hold about 600kg of pulling effort.

required with no additional load penalty. However, too many pickets or pins loosen the ground reducing the effective hold. Ideally, several holdfasts should be used spread apart in a fan arrangement.

If it is not possible to set a picket all the way into the ground they should be at an angle such that the rope pulls down the shaft towards the ground. This strategy can fail if the picket moves to a vertical position and is the reason for chaining several in line. It is important to remember that even though the holding power is increased all the power is still felt through the first picket and attachments. All joints and lashings must still be capable of transmitting the pulling force.

DEADMAN ANCHORS

A deadman is a buried object and is more effective, though much harder work than using multiple pickets. The bearing area is the effective area bearing against the soil, excluding the cable trench. A 3ft long log of 6in diameter with a cable trench of minimal width (say 20mm) gives a bearing area of approx 1½sqft, and will provide a hold against around 910kg (2,000lb) of pull if buried 3 feet deep. The trench should be back-filled unless the walls are very firm. Vertical beams can be set in to act as a wide group of pickets and increase the effective depth and bearing area. A log placed on the surface prevents the cable cutting into the ground, but increases the effective pulling angle with a greater tendency to lift the anchoring device out of the ground. Keeping the cable out of contact with the ground reduces the fouling and eventual cleaning and lubricating task.

The unusual units (kg/ft^2) are used as it is easier to estimate a square foot than fractions of a square metre. Chart 1 can be used to assess other dimensions and pulling angles as required. This has been extrapolated from the table data and provides a wider range of useful information.

A 16in wheel with 225/75 tyre has a bearing area of approx 1.8ft^2 edge on, so if buried 3 feet down will offer a hold against 1,220kg (2,700lb) at 14°. This can be compared with the effective hold provided by two linked 1–1 holdfasts of 1,260kg (2,775lb) in undisturbed earth. It is obviously easier to set 4 pickets than dig a hole 3 feet deep by 3 feet square to take a wheel. Alternatively, if the wheel can be buried vertically with the top 3 feet down and side on with a spar across the diameter to anchor a rope, it can hold a pull of approximately 7,200kg (16,000lb) at 3°. If all else fails a shovel and the spare wheel can be very useful!

The chart can also be used to give an estimate of the amount of effort required to extract a well-bogged casualty. For example, a deadman can withstand a pull of 200kg per sqft area at 11° on something buried around 1½ft down in undisturbed earth. In wet clay, sand or bog the effective hold is about half this (Table 1). A vehicle bogged to its axles and chassis will have a bearing area of approximately 4sqft for the wheels and another 4sqft for the axles and

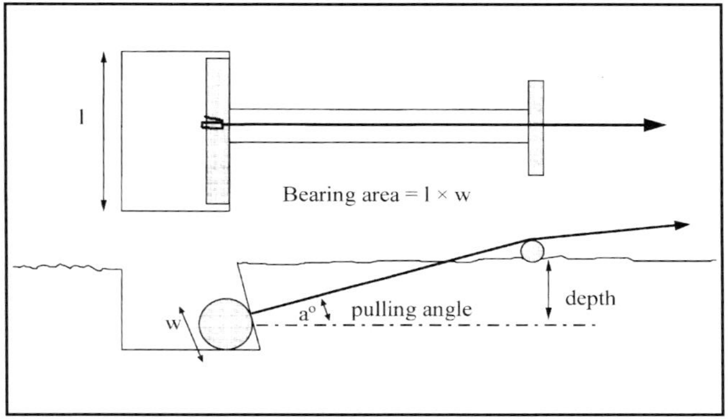

Figure 5

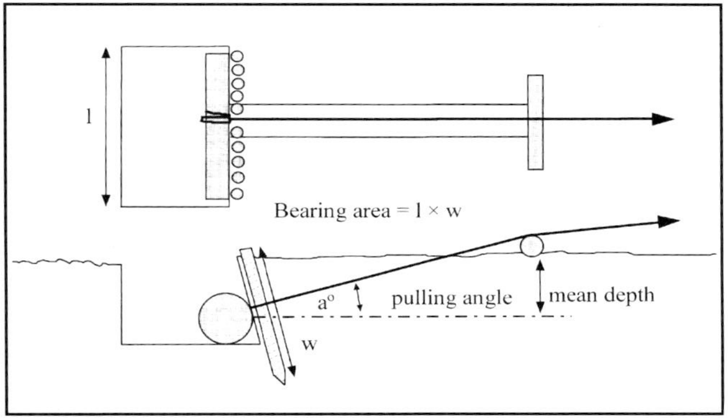

Figure 6

Inclination of pull of projected area from horizontal per unit bearing area

Mean depth		Vertical		45° (1 in 1)		27° (1 in 2)		18° (1 in 3)		14° (1 in 4)	
(ft)	(m)	(lb/ft^2)	(kg/ft^2)	(lb/ft^2)	(kg/ft^2)	(lb/ft^2)	(kg/ft^2)	(lb/ft^2)	(kg/ft^2)	(lb/ft^2)	(kg/ft^2)
3	0.92	600	272	950	431	1300	590	1450	658	1500	681
4	1.22	1050	477	1750	795	2200	999	2600	1180	2700	1226
5	1.53	1700	772	2800	1271	3600	1634	4000	1816	4100	1861
6	1.83	2400	1090	3800	1725	5100	2315	5800	2633	6000	2724
7	2.14	3200	1453	5100	2315	7000	3178	8000	3632	8400	3814

Table 2

suspension parts. There will be some suction due to flat surfaces such as fuel tank and floors, and probably a further 4sqft for chassis sections, making about 13sqft in total. The mean depth is around 1½ft and the pulling angle around 11°, so it can be seen that a pull of about 2,600kg (5,700lb) is required. This represents the effort involved in getting the casualty moving which may also be able to assist with its own power. Once moving, the drag is likely to ease particularly if ladders or lifting devices are in use; thus the task progressively requires less effort.

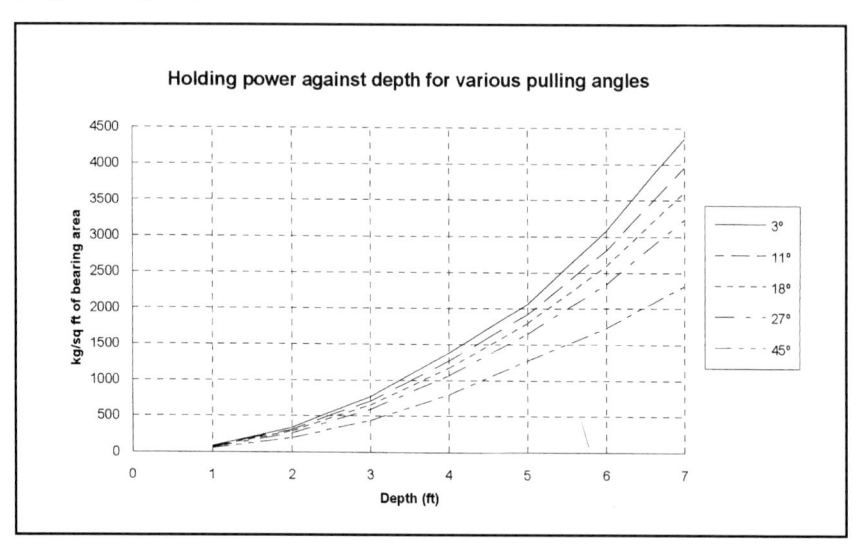

Chart 1

Deadman anchor using spare wheel, before backfilling. Note use of chain to avoid winch cable becoming contaminated with soil.

WINCHING

The most important considerations here are capacity of winch, rope and holdfast, along with an estimate of the required pull. This is not the same as the dead-weight of the vehicle, which is only true if suspended from the ground. Pulling effort depends on the coefficient of friction along with the weight and slope angle (see Appendix B). Snatch blocks can be used to increase the effective pull or change direction. A 38m length of rope may look impressive when stretched out, but doubled round a snatch block it's not quite the same! It is important to remember never to run wire cable through bare hands as there may be broken strands protruding, and never to step over, cross or stand in line of any laden rope. Any snatching of a heavy load on a winch cable should be avoided if at all possible, as the cable – which has no stretch – may break, the drum collapse or the winch mounts shear – all of which can have disastrous consequences. If a rope fails, it will fly back with potentially catastrophic results.

If a tree is being used as an anchor, wide strops should be used to avoid damaging the bark and hence killing it. Do not wrap them round as this will also cause damage: a single loop behind is sufficient and even if it does damage the bark it will not on its own kill the tree. When attaching ropes to a casualty it is sensible to use a lashing ring, otherwise known as jate rings, masterlinks and so on. This enables additional ropes to be added or taken off without loosening the only rope that may be preventing the casualty from falling back.

Friction modifies the load being pulled and is dependant on several factors: weight, surfaces and angles a casualty is being pulled over. Charts showing pulling effort, expressed as a percentage of load weight, against angle of slope are shown in Appendix B. The effect of friction is that the load appears heavier than it is. For example, dragging a vehicle up a 45° (1 in 1) sticky wet clay surface with no assistance from the casualty requires a pull of 110% (1.1 times) of the casualty weight. Translated, this means that a 2,000kg casualty requires a pull of 2,200kg.

Snatch blocks reduce the line pull, but at the expense of reduced speed and distance. They are subject to friction (in their bearings) and a rule of thumb is to reduce the theoretical advantage by 8% per sheave used. The load and winch generate reactionary forces which both operate through the block mounting along with an extra load experienced at the winch due to friction. So, a single block providing an acute offset pull to a separately mounted winch will entail a force at the winch of 1.08 times the load; the block mounting will then need to hold 2.08 times the casualty load. If the winch is attached to the casualty, the mounting load is equal to the load being pulled. Figure 7 shows mounting loads and pulling factors for various configurations of snatch and sheave blocks. The load is the casualty dead weight modified by

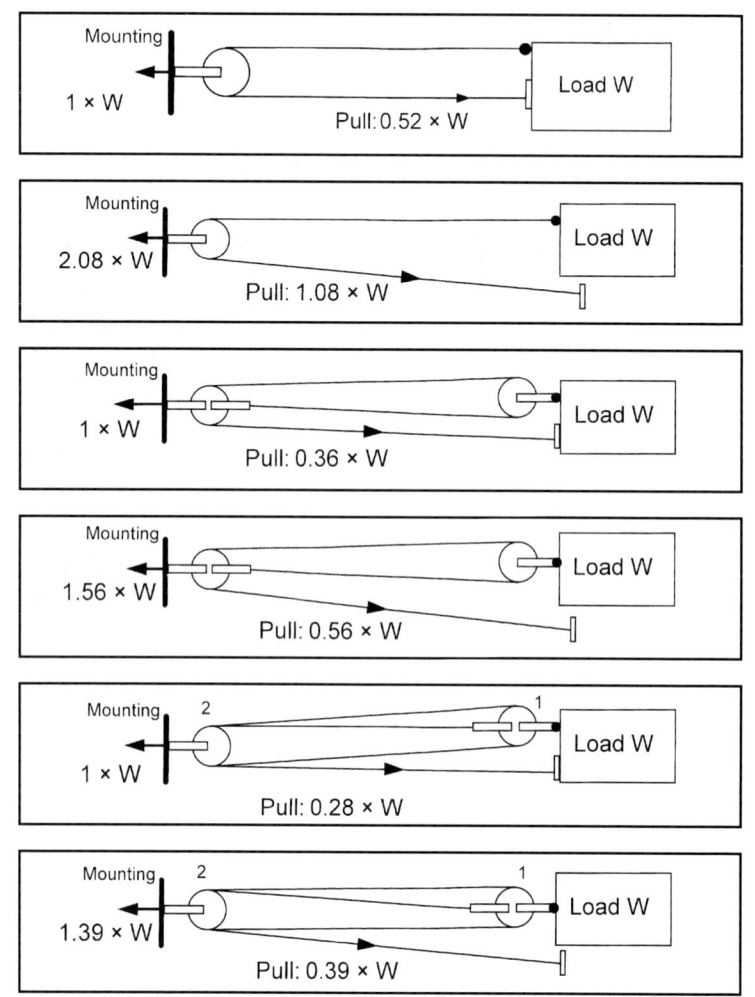

Figure 7

friction and slope as necessary. These figures assume that the angle between the two ropes is very small – less than 5° which would be the case if the rope hook was attached to the winch vehicle.

For 'recreational' or light duty use it is customary to fit electric winches. These are generally lighter and much simpler to install than mechanically or hydraulically driven ones. Because of the very high battery currents required and consequent motor overheating, they are only rated for intermittent use. This can easily be for less than quarter of an hour before the battery needs to be recharged and allowed to recover, as well as letting the motor cool down. For continuous or frequent use mechanical winches are the preferred choice. These are driven direct from the engine or from the PTO via a mechanical or hydraulic link. They can be obtained with higher capacities than the available electric winches, but are significantly heavier and require a better standard of servicing.

Correct use of a tree strop.

Adjustable chain being used as a bridle. The tow brackets are mounted through to the chassis, not the bumper.

The consequences of winching off-centre, to be avoided if at all possible. Use a lashing ring to secure casualty to a fixed anchor before respooling winch rope.

Use of electric winches should be undertaken sparingly depending on how the battery has been wired. A typical winch can draw in excess of 400 amps and a battery will not last long. Even a high capacity alternator will not be much help and it is obvious that the engine should be kept running (until the charge falls to a level too low to keep the fuel or ignition running) with winching time kept to a minimum. Ideally, a second battery charged through split charge diodes should be used.

All drum winches suffer from a variable torque output due to the increased effective drum diameter as each layer is wound on. The difference between an empty and nearly full drum is quite large. For example, the Superwinch Husky has a bottom layer pull of 3,860kg (8,500lb) and a top layer pull of 2,542kg (5,600lb). It may be that in difficult conditions the only use of such a winch is for the first two or three layers. Often a fixed winch will be mounted at the wrong end, in the mud or against a rock, and this is where a portable winch is handy. Unfortunately, to be portable they are of a light weight and restricted to low power devices of low capacity. They also require long power cables and sockets and have a limited rope capacity due to the smaller drum. Appendix D lists some data for Superwinch products.

There are two gearing mechanisms commonly used for mechanical/electric winches. One uses a worm gear and the other a planetary gear or conventional spur gear. Worm gears are inherently self-braking as they cannot be turned by the drum being unwound by a load. Winches with this type of gearing are most suitable when it is necessary to have a long controlled pay-out, such as when assisting a controlled descent down a steep slope. The planetary or any other reduction gear mechanism must use a separate braking system. For simplicity, most use an automatic system with an angled braking material which only operates in the reverse direction. Because of this, powered paying-out cannot be continued for long without overheating the brake (which is usually the inside of the cable drum). This will also increase current consumption to similar levels as for winching-in. Since the motor must be capable of overcoming this automatic braking effect, the brake itself cannot hold more than about 60% of the maximum pulling capacity. In extreme cases this means that it may not be possible to stop winching without the load running away again. Some winches use a ratchet-and-pawl mechanism to hold a reversing load, but even more care must be taken with these to avoid any sudden loads or snatching. The use of non-worm automatically braked winches should be restricted to winding-in applications only.

When using a winch, always wear strong gloves when handling the cable.

An alternative is a hand-winch such as a Tirfor. These can be used anywhere from any direction, and thus are not restricted to a frontal pull and can be used with any length of rope as can a capstan winch. This type of winch operates on a 'hand-to-hand' principle with self-tightening jaws in a similar manner to pop-rivet pliers, and the ropes are specially constructed to resist the clamping effect of the jaws. Conventional ropes should never be used in such machines as the normal 'fail-safe' attributes will be severely compromised. Because of the rope construction the minimum bending diameters of this type are greater than for normal wire rope, so should never be used with normal snatch blocks.

Model	Rope diameter		Minimum bend diameter	
	(in)	(mm)	(in)	(mm)
T508	5/16	8.2	6	152
T516	7/16	11.3	8	203
T532	5/8	16.3	9	229

Table 3

There are two models of Tirfor each in three pull capacities. The ones usually employed for self-recovery purposes are the T5 series rated with a 5:1 safety factor. Of these perhaps the T516 is the most useful, having a lifting capacity (SWL) of 1,600kg and pulling capacity of 2,500kg. The rope used has a breaking strain of 8,145kg. It requires an effort at the rated SWL of 40kg to move the rope 42mm per operating cycle; thus it can be seen that it provides a 40:1 mechanical advantage. The T532 provides a 71:1 advantage against which is the greater physical size, weight and much reduced pull distance per cycle (23mm). If a load is impossible for one man to move, the use of snatch blocks – of correct pulley diameter – is advised. Extra manpower may easily exceed the SWL! Tirfor winches are rated with a safety factor of 5, but increasing the load also increases the effort required. With this safety factor, a T516 is theoretically capable of pulling 12,500kg, but would require an effort at the lever of 313kg! So, in addition to being the SWL, the rating also gives an indication of what one person can move. If overloaded, a protective shear pin fails thus preventing the machine from being used to pull in. This is a fail-safe mechanism and does not prevent a controlled pay-out or lowering to a safe position.

It should be obvious from Figure 7 that any winch mountings on a vehicle must be secure and substantial. Towbars are rated to pull 3,500kg with a ball (and if designed for BSAU24 4-bolt mountings for NATO and similar jaws, 4,070kg). Hanging a portable winch of rating 4,000lb (1,816kg) on a towball mount and using it with a snatch block can easily generate forces on the tow bar of 3,500kg, so care should be taken! Similarly, if you are winching a dead 2-tonne vehicle from sticky clay up a 45° slope and using a tow ball on another vehicle to carry a snatch block, the load on the ball will be 2.08 × 2000 × 1.1 = 4,576kg! This is well over the safe design rating.

One important point to note with all drum winches is to ensure that the rope always pulls in line with the vehicle. Even with a roller fairlead any offset pulling angles will cause the rope to pile up at one end or other of the drum. The rope will bunch, fouling the mounting frame or casing and probably trap itself between windings thus causing breakages or kinks. If the rope slips under these conditions the resultant snatch can damage the winch, vehicles and rope.

Most vehicles are designed to travel forwards over the ground or obstacles. If a vehicle is being recovered backwards out of a hole, if at all possible the winch rope should be attached by a two-leg sling or bridle to the axle, as close to the wheels as possible. It is quite easy, especially in boggy ground, for the body to be supported and the axle to drop down to the maximum spring extension. This will catch behind the ground being 'bulldozed' up. Unless the axle can cut through the ground, the consequences can be an axle ripped off its mountings. This will also push the gearbox and engine forwards, at best bending the rear propshaft and at worst twisting the chassis mountings. The

A Tirfor can be used from any direction: front-mounted winches are no help when going backwards.

larger electric winches can easily generate a pull in excess of 7 tonnes force when used with a snatch block. If a casualty will not move with a single winch then it will need to have the obstructing ground dug away to assist with free movement of any low hanging parts.

The maximum load likely to be imposed on a winch for self-recovery is around 1.2 times the vehicle deadweight. Fitting a winch with double the deadweight capacity will be sufficient for virtually all purposes. This capacity should be that of a full drum and not the maximum pull as usually quoted by the manufacturers on the bare drum. A winch with 30 metres of rope is not much use if the only available anchoring point is a few metres away and the the pulling effort required is close to the maximum rating. Snatch blocks become an essential accessory, but remember the loads being imposed on all the mountings and ensure they are strong enough!

Everything in place and ready to start. The complete wincher at work and play.

BRIDGING

Strictly speaking, bridging is a specialist subject. However, bearing in mind some basic principles it is possible to make some effective temporary bridges using logs or other similar materials; caution, as ever, is the watchword. Routes requiring bridges should be avoided if possible. By definition a bridge crosses a gap or hole and it is therefore possible to fall in!

It is desirable that whatever material is used is not too flexible. The ensuing rotation at the ends may well lift any restraints and make the structure unstable. The carrying capacity is strongly influenced by the fixings used at the ends and the elasticity and dimensions (predominantly the vertical depth) of the material used. This is described in more detail in Appendix C and later in this chapter. Effective materials can be readily found: logs, hollow metal sections, I-section girders or similar. Logs found lying around can be partially rotten and even freshly-cut timber may contain flaws. If in doubt, build a trial structure just above the ground where any failure will not create a hazard and try it out first. Bark-covered logs can be particularly dangerous. While bark is rough and offers good grip it does have an unfortunate habit of peeling away and should be removed if that is likely to happen. It is vitally important that when using simple and temporary bridges a guide is used to watch where the wheels are being placed: even with the best will in the world it is easy to slip off – with the obvious consequences. It may also be wise to build in a spacer to help maintain the correct gap between the spans.

Metals are rated in terms of their elasticity. Within the elastic range the material should return to its original shape when the load is removed. The elastic limit – the point at which permanent deformation takes place – is what governs any load limits and minimum breaking force (MBF). Intermittent loads close to the MBF shorten a structure's working life. When materials are loaded there are microscopic changes to the internal structure and with frequent high loads these changes become bigger, more permanent and work-hardened. As a result the elastic limit reduces and failure becomes more likely. For practical vehicle-based purposes, bridges need to be as light as possible, which means that working loads are much closer to the MBF. Consequently, lightweight structures need frequent examination with scrapping if there is any sign of permanent deformation. Timber, in particular, can fail without warning or significant prior bending especially when dry. Rapid movement across a bridge can increase the effective loading and it is wisest to cross temporary structures slowly, which also assists with accurate wheel positioning. This increased load can be up to twice the deadweight.

A simple way of establishing a safe load is based on the following table and formula for solid rectangular beams of various materials:

Material	c	End supports	k
Mild Steel	5.517	One fixed, other end loaded	1
Cast Iron	3.625	One fixed, load distributed	1
Aluminium Alloy	1.889	Both supported load in centre	4
English Oak	1.182	Both supported load distributed	8
Red Pine	1.025	Both fixed, load in centre	6
Fir (Spruce)	0.946	Both fixed load distributed	12
Yellow Pine	0.788		

Table 4

For solid rectangular section:
Minimum Breaking Force in kg $= \dfrac{breadth \times depth^2}{span} \times c \times k$, (dimensions in mm).

It is safer to try to bridge gaps of less than the wheelbase when using temporary structures so that the whole weight of the vehicle will not be on the structure at any one time. If spans greater than the wheelbase are to be constructed and if the vehicle weight is assumed to be in the centre, further safety factors are built in as any structure can sustain higher loads provided they are distributed across the span.

A readily portable bridge section will be shorter than the wheelbase of most off-road vehicles which means that each span will only carry one wheel at a time. An estimate must be made of the maximum single wheel load to be supported taking account of weight distribution (see Appendix F for some

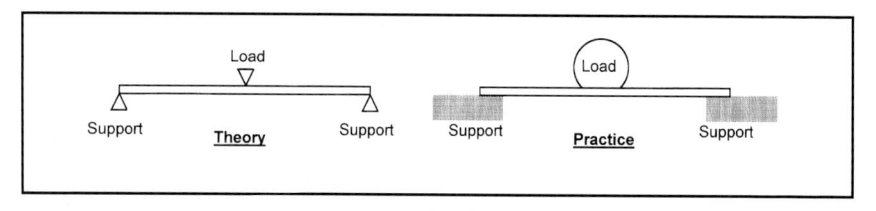

Figure 8

typical figures). For safety, ready-made structures should be capable of carrying the maximum feasible loading in order to provide a margin for emergency loads or when the user forgets the capacity! Good practice dictates fixing the ends to pickets with an overlap of the end supports. Assuming that the span width is the length of the spars to be used, ignoring the supporting overlap along with a point load rather than the tyre footprint, provides an additional safety margin.

For example: a 2m piece of rectangular spruce 130mm wide × 130mm deep is to be used to form a bridge across a 1.75m gap, with loose ends supported by the ground. Applying these values into the formula above gives a breaking load of 4,157kg in the centre of the span. With a factor of safety of 4 this gives a safe load of 1,039kg per span.

Examination of the formula shows that the MBF is more dependent on the depth than the width. This means that it is not a simple matter to convert from one cross-section to another. These relationships can be deduced by comparing motions of area which are listed in Appendix C. A modified formula for circular section is:

$$\text{solid round section: } MBF(\text{kg}) = \frac{diameter^3}{span} \times c \times k \times 0.589,$$

$$\text{or: } \quad diameter = 1.193 \times \sqrt[3]{\frac{span \times MBF}{c \times k}};$$

where dimensions are in mm, with c and k taken from Table 4 as before.

This shows that a circular pole of 155mm diameter (0.076m² csa) spruce will hold a similar load (4,159kg) before failing as does the 130mm × 130mm (0.039m² csa) beam.

To increase the load-bearing area several lengths of timber could be lashed together. Thus narrower timbers could be used, but additional safety factors would need to be introduced as the effective strength would depend very much on the lashings, particularly if the load could not be distributed evenly across all the parallel timbers. Use of the *diameter* formula for solid round section above helps. However, it is not a simple matter of dividing a single diameter by the number of pieces. Instead it requires the **load** to be divided across each of the timbers, remembering that the tyre footprint may not be supported equally, and then calculating the diameters for each spar with proportionate loading. The spars should ideally be the same diameter to avoid unequal loading and bending, shown in Table 5, which assumes supported ends and a central point load.

Yellow pine of 2500kg MBF per side span	1000mm	1500mm	2000mm	3000mm	4000mm
min dia one piece per side span (FS 2)	1 × 110mm	1 × 126mm	1 × 140mm	1 × 160mm	1 × 175mm
min dia two pieces per side span (FS 2)	2 × 88mm	2 × 100mm	2 × 110mm	2 × 126mm	2 × 140mm

Yellow pine of 3000kg MBF per side span	1000mm	1500mm	2000mm	3000mm	4000mm
min dia one piece per side span (FS 2)	1 × 118mm	1 × 135mm	1 × 148mm	1 × 170mm	1 × 187mm
min dia two pieces per side span (FS 2)	2 × 94mm	2 × 107mm	2 × 118mm	2 × 135mm	2 × 148mm

Table 5

Saving a lot of digging! Bridging ladders do more than cross gaps.

It is good practice to assume that one of these parallel timbers will fail and then to recalculate loads accordingly. As an alternative, ready-made bridge spans can be carried. These will be bulky and heavy, but could readily double as traction ladders. Unfortunately, when planning an expedition through unknown territory it may not be possible to know in advance what gaps will need to be bridged. Use of general-purpose ladders linked together involves joints which may weaken the structure at the very point maximum strength is required. The complete assembled structure must be capable of carrying the full required load: two lengths of capacity at 1 tonne each will, if joined in line, carry less than 500kg! When calculating bridge loads, the overall gap is the span length and the supporting overhang should be ignored. Appendix C contains tables and data showing breaking strengths, weights and other parameters for some common steel cross-sections that could be used for bridging purposes, along with detailed formulae.

Centre of gravity is also something to be taken into account: if the two bridge spans are not on the same horizontal level, the load will be increased on the downhill side. As much care should be taken if this is the scenario as

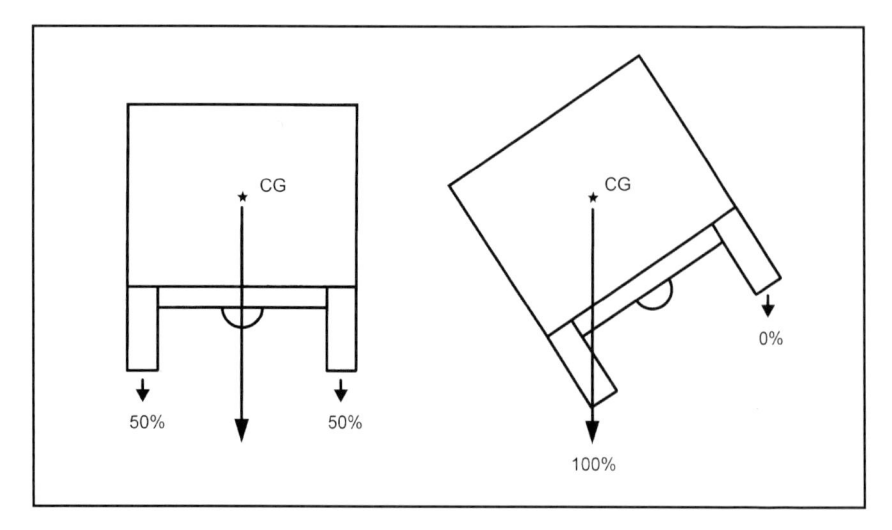

Figure 9

when traversing a side slope. In some cases a side slope of much less than 45° may well mean that one bridge span is effectively carrying the full weight of the vehicle. Thus any bridge section should ideally be able to carry safely the full vehicle weight, with as little bending as possible as this would increase the side tilt, with possibly disastrous results. In practice, this would make any ready-made temporary structure too unwieldy to carry and means that gaps crossing a level camber are the only ones suitable for simple bridges. It would be good practice to level-off approach and departure cambers if at all possible, consistent with minimizing damage to the ground.

TRACTION AIDS

As the name suggests, traction aids are a means of increasing the amount of tractive effort that can be imparted in order to keep or start a vehicle moving, and they can take many forms. It is possible to use rags, blankets, twigs and branches and so on, but they are not very effective. A boggy piece of ground could be bridged, but that demands considerable effort and materials that may not be available. Simple plastic mats can be bought and even rubber car mats can be used. Flexible materials do not reduce ground pressure and are invariably useless unless the soft ground is shallow with a hard sub-surface and the mat offers grip to the tyres. A far more successful alternative is to use a metal structure such as a sand, bog or traction ladder, or the 'PSP' (perforated steel planking) used by the military for constructing airfields.

Obviously the more rigid or solid metal devices have some weight and tend to be awkward to load and carry. To be convenient and readily transportable they should be made of simple and light materials, without hooks or sharp edges. Being light they are prone to bending and should only be used when supported. Unless specifically designed as such, they are NOT bridging

Winching onto traction ladders.

Use of an airbag to lift a casualty enabling the hole to be filled or traction device to be put in position.

devices and typical traction ladders will have a maximum unsupported load of up to a few hundred kg. In some cases this may be sufficient to bridge small holes or very uneven snow and bog.

Traction ladders are simple and should ideally be placed under a wheel with the vehicle jacked up. Trying to push them under a spinning wheel is potentially dangerous and should only be done with extreme caution. Several lengths can be laid together to cover a wide section of ground. Care should be taken to ensure that the ends do not pivot round and jam under the chassis. If necessary, lengths of rope can be used to tie them to the vehicle to simplify the job of recovering them after use, particularly if they are likely to become buried. However, if this is done they will act as a drag and may prevent further progress. It may be preferable to tie a coloured rope or cloth to identify them for later recovery instead.

Other traction aids frequently used are snowchains and studs. Chains need to be fitted to the wheels at the time of need, often in cold, wet and windy conditions and must also be removed on return to any hard surface. They can be used to good effect in mud as well as snow. Studs are only of use on ice and must be properly inserted into appropriate tyres. However, many countries do not permit their use, as on Tarmac studs damage both road and tyre and when they come out they fly around like bullets! Alternatives to snowchains could be short lengths of rope, assuming that the wheels are slotted. Towing chain could also be used provided that the ends are securely lashed inside the wheel and away from contact with the axle and suspension. Rope will not damage Tarmac roads, but it is not as tough as steel chain and cannot provide the same level of surface penetration, but it is a useful last-ditch alternative.

TRACTION

Tractive effort available depends on the ground condition, tyre condition and type. As a guide, the horizontal force at which slipping occurs can be found from:

$$F_m = \mu_o R_w$$

Where μ_o is the coefficient of adhesion and R_w the load per wheel.

	μ_o		μ_o
Asphalt/concrete, dry	0.8–0.9	Clay, dry	0.5–0.6
Asphalt/concrete, wet	0.4–0.7	Sand, loose	0.3–0.4
Gravel, rolled, dry	0.6–0.7	Ice, dry	0.2
Gravel, loose, wet	0.3–0.5	Ice, wet	0.1

Table 6

A wheel laden with 600kg on loose sand will be able to transmit up to 240kg of force. Therefore, a typical 4 x 4 will be able to generate 960kg of tractive effort or pulling force before wheelspin occurs.

The resistance of a vehicle to motion is made up of rolling resistance, gradient force and aerodynamic drag. For recovery purposes drag can be ignored. Gradient force is dealt with under the appendix on Friction which takes account of the slope and vehicle weights – effectively, the amount of effort required to move a vehicle up the incline. If the vehicle is on level ground there is no gradient force required, but it should be remembered that gradient also includes small steps and slopes, climbing out of ruts and so on.

The rolling resistance of a vehicle is the amount of force necessary to keep it moving:

$$F_r = C_r mg \text{ newtons}$$

where F_r is the rolling resistance, C_r the coefficient of rolling resistance taken from the following table, m the mass of the vehicle and g the coefficient of gravity.

	C_r		C_r
Asphalt or concrete, new	0.01	Gravel, rolled, new	0.02
Asphalt or concrete, old	0.02	Gravel, loose, worn	0.04
Cobbles, small, new	0.01	Soil, medium hard	0.08
Cobbles, large, worn	0.03	Sand	0.1–0.3

Table 7

For example, a 2.4-tonne 4x4 vehicle on soft sand requires 0.3 × 2400 × 9.81 = 7063kN (720kgf) to keep it moving, or about 180kgf per wheel. If our vehicle was only two-wheel drive, the maximum tractive force available would be 480kgf, and it would go nowhere!

If a moving vehicle in sand is watched closely, the wheels will be seen to be slipping. The amount of slip and forward momentum depends on the ability of the tyres to continue climbing out of the hole it is making for itself, hence creating the rut. As with any material, the 'strength' is dependant on how the particles adhere to one another, so sand clearly has low adhesion (particularly if dry). However, if the sand is compacted it affords much better grip and is less prone to creating ruts. As with pickets used as ground anchors, any cleats or tyre protrusions – such as heavy treads – will break the surface thus making the wheel more prone to spinning and digging in. This is the reason why sand tyres are all but treadless as they compact the sand particles and minimize breaking the surface. Cleated tyres are most effective if the ground material is sticky enough not to be broken up.

The reason traction aids can be so effective is that as well as spreading the load across a much bigger area reducing ground pressure, they also spread the tractive effort over that larger area. Our 240kgf effort would normally be spread over about 1sqft (2580kgf/m^2). Using a traction mat to spread that force over a greater area ensures that the effort being transmitted to the ground surface is below the tractive limit. If we required 300kgf per wheel (3225kgf/m^2), applying that to an area of 2sqft would halve the tractive force per square foot of ground area and wheelspin would be avoided. Reducing the ground pressure also has the effect of reducing the susceptibility to sinking in wet or boggy ground.

LIFTING

Lifting is used for many purposes – most obviously, to get out of a hole or change a wheel. Vehicles should be lifted to enable placement of traction ladders or other objects under the wheels thus clearing chassis parts from contact with the ground. The basic rules are to watch and be careful, particularly if using high-lift jacks. A jacked vehicle weighing 2 tons can be very unstable, and more so if it has a laden roof rack.

The usual devices for off-road use are the well known 'Jackall', 'Hi Lift' and also airbags. High-lift jacks and others of a similar design can further double as effective winches, but of low mechanical advantage. Airbags can fit anywhere, providing there are no sharp protrusions or hot parts such as exhausts. Care must be taken when inflating them with a diesel vehicle as attempts to over-

Not quite as easy as this suggests! High-lift jack used as a short-haul winch. Note use of adjustable chains.

inflate will cover the operator in a cloud of sticky soot when releasing the pipe! They also require exhaust systems to be in good condition with no leaks.

Vehicles raised on high-lift devices will usually have only two wheels remaining in contact with the ground and will slew very readily – which can be used to good effect to get clear of ruts. Don't get in the way and do use chocks wherever appropriate. If there is any danger of the casualty rolling away or slewing it should be lashed to a holdfast, and if a handwinch is used to lash the casualty any movement can be easily controlled. One difficulty with mechanical high-lift jacks is often a lack of suitable locating points which should ideally be socketed to prevent the casualty sliding on the lifting toe. However, if you are prepared to accept bodywork damage they can be put to use almost anywhere. Ninety/One Ten Land Rovers use a tubular socket as standard and adaptors are available to enable use of high-lift jacks on these proper jacking points. A hazard with these adaptors is that there is an increased leverage on the jackshaft due to the bearing area being moved away from the centre line of the main beam. Consequently, the jack capacity should be derated. If there is then any increased risk of instability, it is preferable that the normal jack toe be used under a suitably robust part of the chassis.

In use, a high-lift jack operates as a variable eccentrically loaded strut. The load-carrying part is offset from the main beam by about 100mm and up to 185mm with a 90/110 adaptor. This load positioning severely derates the beam capacity which reduces in non-linear proportion to the distance between foot and lifting toe. In addition, the holes also reduce the effective cross-sectional area and hence strength. The effect of loading a strut in this manner causes it to curve outwards as shown in Figure 10. If the jack were able to carry the load vertically in line with the beam it would support up to about 14,000kg before collapsing.

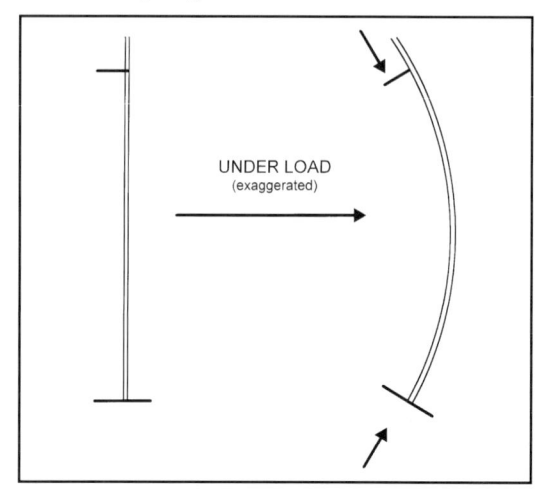

Figure 10

Chart 2 illustrates predicted yield points for various loads and heights, based on a yield stress limit of $300GN/m^2$ and clearly shows that the capacity is reduced with high lifts. These limits are those at which the beam will stay bent. Even if the beam doesn't yield, the risk of the foot or lifting toe sliding is significantly increased. Since a low yield stress figure was used, and considering that only part of the weight of a vehicle is being lifted, use of these upper limits provides a safety margin. Particular care should be taken when using 90/110 adaptors, as the theoretical maximum capacity of the jack is no more than 2,000kg (4,400lb).

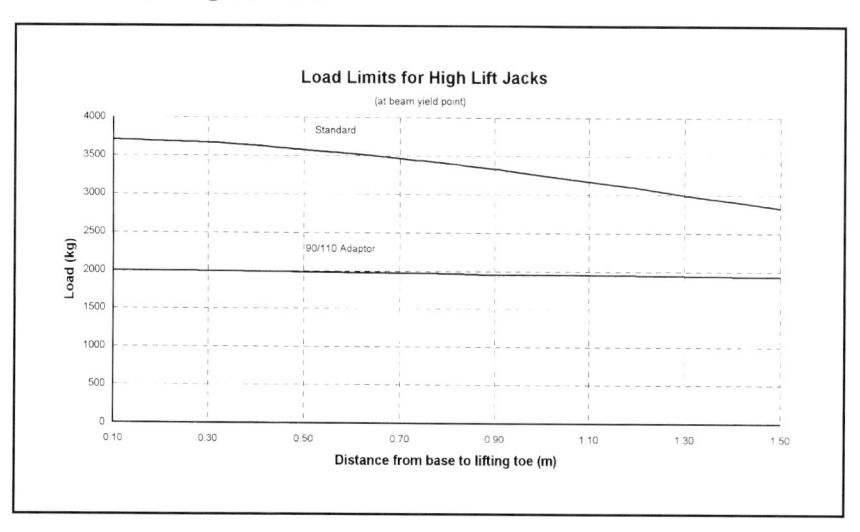

Load Limits for High Lift Jacks
(at beam yield point)

[Chart showing Load (kg) vs Distance from base to lifting toe (m), with "Standard" curve decreasing from ~4000kg at 0.10m to ~2700kg at 1.50m, and "90/110 Adaptor" curve roughly flat around 2000kg]

Chart 2

Multi-leg slings are more usually associated with cranes. However, they can be put to effective use as bridles when towing or pulling, to help spread a load across more than one lashing point or when damage to the casualty prevents use of single point attachments. In some cases it may be necessary to use a spreader bar. All of these slings require some form of link or loop ring attachment to the pulling device. If the angle between the legs is not zero the load capacity is reduced, as shown in Table 8. In all cases the maximum SWL is dictated by the weakest link in the equipment used.

Another useful function of a mechanical high-lift jack is to break tyre beads, either by squeezing between the foot and a heavy object (such as your vehicle) or a top-clamp adaptor. Top clamps provide a means of attaching chains or ropes when used as winches and should be employed in preference to shackles. Suitable shackles with pins small enough to go through the holes in the beam are only rated at around 500 to 700kg. With the jack capable of generating forces in excess of 3,600kg the small shackles are easily bent.

Load limits for two-leg slings

Capacity (kg) Single leg	Angle between legs				
	0°	30°	60°	90°	120°
500	1000	966	866	707	500
750	1500	1449	1299	1061	750
1000	2000	1932	1673	1414	1000
1500	3000	2898	2598	2121	1500
2000	4000	3864	3464	2828	2000
2500	5000	4830	4330	3535	2500
Load reduction factor		0.966	0.866	0.707	0.5

Table 8

Single-leg adjustable chain sling. This makes a very effective bridle and can be used when there is danger of damaging ropes or strops. The 7mm chain shown here has a 6280kg minimum breaking load.

TOWING

This is a relatively simple operation, hazards here relating to the difficulties of steering and braking. Ideally, a rigid tow should be used to enable the towing vehicle to brake the combination, but this can be hampered by a lack of suitable mounting points on the front of the casualty.

Snatching any towed load should be avoided at all costs unless an elastic rope is used; considerable damage can be done to both vehicles if insufficient care is taken.

If a rigid bar is available it should be used with a rotating hitch (military style pintle) on the towing vehicle. The other end should be well secured to the casualty, ideally on another military pintle and preferably in the centre line. The pivot locking pin should be removed allowing the pintle to rotate. Military Land Rovers have lifting/towing eyes which are installed for use with A-frames and thus avoid the need for a driver in the casualty.

Polypropylene rope is cheap but 'dead' with no give and is really only suitable for lashing and steady towing on Tarmac or a smooth surface.

Standard plait nylon and natural fibres (such as manila) have a small amount of give, and can be used for most purposes including with a capstan winch, but are not suitable for snatch recovery unless the loads are relatively light.

Kinetic Energy Recovery Ropes permit snatch recovery by applying the built-up kinetic energy of the towing vehicle to be applied to the casualty in a controlled manner. The ropes are specially constructed with a more elastic material (usually nylon) and a multi-plait geometry. As the towing vehicle extends the rope and is slowed down, the energy is transferred to the rope and hence the casualty, until sufficient is – hopefully – applied to overcome the inertia and friction.

In principle, a sudden application of pulling force to a casualty will overcome inertia and other obstructions more easily. However, it is far more likely to damage both vehicles as well as the rope. Applying the force in a controlled manner with a KERR avoids this but requires space for a run-up, which is an additional problem.

A well-bogged 2-tonne vehicle can easily present an effective load equal to its weight, especially if there is a slope or rut to climb. Another 2-tonne moving vehicle will impart an effective pull of at least 3 or 4 times its dead weight increasing in proportion to the square of its speed (double the speed and the energy increases by 4 times). Consequently, the total load on the rope can easily be 5 or more times the casualty weight. As a result, a 12-tonne 24mm KERR will be operating very close to its breaking point particularly since most off-road vehicles will have some load and easily weigh more than 2 tonnes. A short KERR will not allow much speed to be built up but is less likely to fail yet can also be used as highly effective shock absorbers between tow chains. A long KERR could easily be overloaded and snap, especially if the fibres are not in good condition.

KERR ropes have a lot of give and should not be used on the road unless they are short. They are unlikely to be any use for lashing or winching due to the stretching – which can be up to around 40% depending on load so that when used to snatch a bogged casualty can extend alarmingly. This has an impact on the route being taken by the recovering vehicle especially if it has to negotiate bends or obstructions.

All ropes have a limited working life, being subject to chafing and chemical attack, particularly those composed from man-made fibres. In addition to the material used, the construction method provides a variable elasticity (except polypropylene). The effect of the material is dependent on whether the fibres can slip over each other. Ropes stretch when loaded, and if the material is rough the fibres will lock on each other inhibiting the free movement which permits stretching. This is one of the reasons why polypropylene has no give. The actual amount of stretch depends on the material and construction, the stretch permitted by the construction being partly dependant on looseness of plait: when loaded this tightens as with a knot; after frequent use there is less flex available and the rope becomes stiff and unyielding. Giving ropes time to recover after being loaded assists in extending their working lives. After a period, all ropes should be discarded as there is an increased risk of failure with small shock loading, due to wear and loss of elasticity. This is particularly important with KERRs as they are inherently used much closer to their breaking limits and should be discarded after no more than half a dozen pulls.

TESTING AND INSPECTION

Safe working load limits are usually set at a quarter of the failure point. The failure point is usually defined at the elastic limit, which is the point at which any additional load results in permanent deformation. Such loads define the Yield Stress limit. Material specifications quote this level and also the Ultimate Tensile Stress at which point the material will fracture (for mild steel this about 30% higher than yield stress). Testing involves loading an object to double its Safe Working Load (half its yield load) and examining it for damage after that load has been removed. Any subsequent stretching or bending should be well within the elastic limit. Equipment for the mining industry and some others is traditionally set at a 5:1 working ratio. These limits are established under Lifting Regulations: any unnecessary loading in excess of the SWL with ensuing personal injury may result in prosecution by the Health and Safety authorities.

For reasons of practicality, it is unlikely that portable devices intended for use under 'emergency' situations would be sufficiently strong to permit infrequent or annual inspection. A simple example is the use of a KERR which is expressly designed to operate in excess of its conventional SWL. In use this will be loaded at or even beyond the theoretical breaking capacity. This means that all of these devices should be inspected prior to being used or carefully observed during use. Obviously, in an emergency, the luxury of over-engineering cannot be relied on and considerable amounts of common sense should be used. Under these conditions portability and practicality dictate that an operator uses whatever equipment may be available. Providing that individuals are not exposed to hazard from any failure of such devices, the loads may go up to the breaking limit. It is for the operator to decide the level of risk imposed on equipment and bystanders: the use of unsafe practices or equipment when alternatives, including seeking further assistance are available, will probably lead to a prosecution.

The following checklist is far from exhaustive, but illustrates particular points to watch, most of which are common sense. However, if in doubt, scrap the item. Authoritative books and courses covering the principles of

Always try out your equipment on a level site to ensure you are familiar with its operation before you need to use it for real. Note that the jack's base is on a piece of wood so as not to sink in the soft ground.

testing are available.

Shackles	No distortion, damaged threads, or cracks around the eyes.
Chains	Links not stretched, cracked or worn. Couplings not worn or loose.
Wire ropes	No wear, corrosion, kinks, broken strands, exposed core.
Fibre ropes	No broken fibres, cuts or nicks, no significant permanent stretching. Splices in good

Ready to go off-roading! All the gear has been cleaned and checked ready for use. Stow it away carefully and know where it all is: you may need it in a hurry and it could be after dark.

Belts/straps/strops	condition and tight. No rotting if natural fibre. Stitching in good condition, no cuts, nicks or stretching.
Hooks/eyes	No cracks, opened-out throats, no distorted eyes.
Beams, arms, spreaders	Straight, no bends, eyes and fittings not distorted or worn.
Mechanisms	No wear, loose or worn bearings, cracks in housings, worn or damaged threads.

Whoops!

GENERAL

This list is not intended to be exhaustive and any operator will undoubtedly be able to come up with many more recommendations.

DO

Use common sense,

Stop and think through a course of action,

Minimize risks,

Respect the environment, including all pedestrians,

Give way to wild life and other animals,

Take your time and analyze what is happening,

Use lashing and guide ropes to help prevent a casualty from moving into a worse position,

Use a lashing ring (jate ring, masterlink etc) when attaching a rope as it enables further ropes to be added or removed without loosening the original,

Use a bridle or two-leg sling if pulling backwards on an axle in difficult conditions,

Dig out obstructing soil to provide a free path,

Use tree strops,

Use sufficient pickets and avoid digging deadman anchors if possible,

Lashing ring in use, allowing multiple attachments without releasing the casualty.

Use the casualty's own motive power to assist but ONLY if it can be done without causing additional ground damage,

Wear gloves when handling ropes, hammers and tools,

Use gravity with a sledge hammer: it should not be pushed down,

Back off shackles ¼ turn after tightening to avoid them jamming after a load has been applied,

Discard and replace worn or damaged tools and equipment on return to civilization,

Keep winches and other mechanisms serviced,

Check your loading list before travelling,

Use the SWL of the weakest link when evaluating lifting or pulling loads,

Use a guide to observe wheel positions when traversing difficult terrain, crossing simple bridges and so on,

Discard worn ropes and KERRs in particular after frequent use.

DON'T

Get in the way of a casualty while it is being moved,

Stand in line with or astride laden winch ropes,

Take unnecessary risks,

Lift higher than necessary,

Continue winching if a casualty appears not to move,

Rely on the axles or bodywork to clear a path through obstructing soil or bog.

A good selection of recovery tools, able to cope with almost anything and weighing about 80kg in total.

Take your time and analyze the situation. You don't want to make an off-road odyssey a journey to the chiropractor.

APPENDIX A – ROPES

These figures should be used as a guide, to which may be added any relevant safety factor, depending on age, condition or construction, which may be unknown. Safe loads are based on factors for lifting purposes.

	Diameter (mm)	Breaking load (kg)	Weight (kg/100m)
Polypropylene	24	4930	26
Manila	24	4570	40
	32	7900	70
Nylon	24	12000	38
	32	20000	67
Nylon multi-plait	24	12000	37
	32	20000	66
Steel 7x19 galvanized wire core	5	1500–1740	10
	6	2160–2510	14
	7	2940–3420	19
	8	3840–4460	24
	9	5200–6060	32
	10	6420–7470	40
	11	7770–9040	48

continued overleaf

Residual strength %

Chemical	Time (hrs)	Nylon	Polypropylene
Hydrochloric Acid	100	0	100
Nitric Acid	100	0	100
Sulphuric Acid	100	0	100
Formic Acid	100	0	100
Acetic Acid	10	85	100
Caustic Soda	100	50	90
Caustic Potash	100	90	90
Trichloroethylene	150	100	80
Carbon Tetrachloride	150	100	100
Benzene	150	100	100
Metacresol	4	0	100
Hydrogen Peroxide	100	0	90

Table 9

APPENDIX B – FRICTION

Friction is a force that offers resistance to motion between surfaces in contact. The coefficient of Friction is a measure of the amount of friction existing between those surfaces. When a load is to be moved horizontally, it is defined as a pull and at any angle away from horizontal is defined as lifting, when a vector addition of the relative forces has to be used.

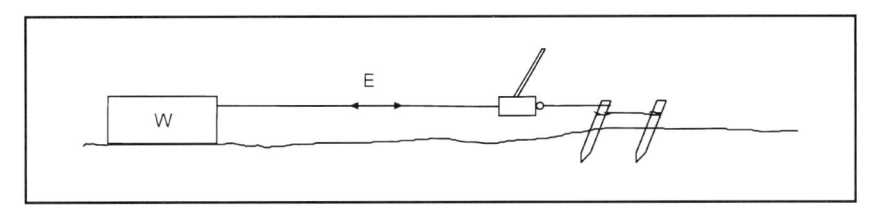

Figure 11

$$E = \mu W;\ \text{for pulling}$$

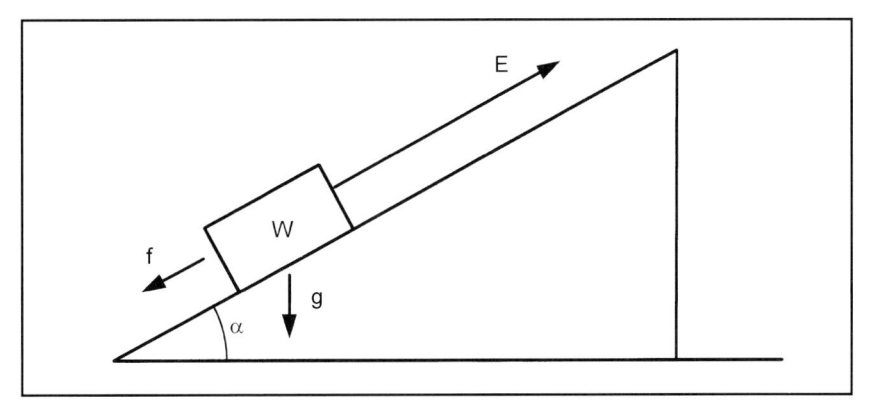

Figure 12

$$E = W(\mu \cos\alpha + \sin\alpha);\ \text{for lifting}$$

where: E is the effort required to move the load,
         W is the weight of the casualty,
         μ is the coefficient of friction,
         α is the angle from horizontal.

Friction imposes an initial resistance to movement, and once moving it reduces slightly to the figures listed. These values can only be established by experiment and can change by a marked amount, particularly in the presence of lubricants and varying conditions of the two surfaces in contact. It is possible for a coefficient to have a value greater than 1, which is unlikely in practice unless the casualty is below the surface level and pulling builds up material in front as with a bulldozer.

COEFFICIENTS of FRICTION

Material	μ	Material	μ
Asphalt/rubber	0.5–0.8	Wheeled load on Tarmac	0.02–0.05
Rubber/steel	0.6–0.9	Iron/stone	0.3–0.7
Rubber/asphalt (wet)	0.25–0.75	Lubricated metal surfaces	0.1–0.2
Rubber/asphalt (dry)	0.5–0.8	Vehicle in wet and clinging clay	0.5
Rubber/concrete (wet)	0.45–0.75	Vehicle in hard wet sand	0.17
Rubber/concrete (dry)	0.6–0.85	Vehicle in soft wet sand	0.2
Dry masonry/brickwork	0.6–0.7	Vehicle in soft dry sand	0.25
Masonry/dry clay	0.5	Vehicle in shallow mud	0.33
Masonry/wet clay	0.3	Vehicle in bog	0.5
Timber/stone	0.4	Vehicle in marsh	0.5
Timber/timber	0.2–0.5	Vehicle on gravel	0.2
Timber/metal	0.2–0.6	Vehicle on grass	0.14

Table 10

The following chart shows pulling effort expressed as a percentage of load and drawn for various coefficients of friction against angle of slope. As can be seen, it is possible to require up to 142% of the casualty weight if the coefficient of friction is 1 on a 45° slope. For example, dragging a vehicle up a 45° (1 in 1) sticky wet clay surface with no assistance from the casualty, requires a pull of 110% or 1.1 times the casualty weight. Translated, this means that a 2,000kg casualty requires a pull of 2,200kg.

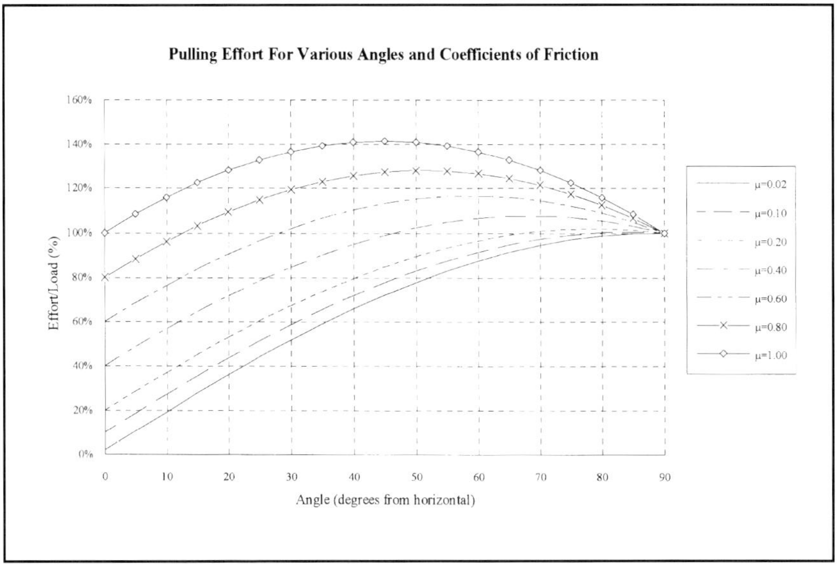

Pulling Effort For Various Angles and Coefficients of Friction
160%
140%
120%
100%
80%
60%
40%
20%
0%
Effort/Load (%)
0
10
20
30
40
50
60
70
80
90
Angle (degrees from horizontal)
μ=0.02
μ=0.10
μ=0.20
μ=0.40
μ=0.60
μ=0.80
μ=1.00

Chart 3

μ	Slope angle at which pulling effort is a maximum
0.02	88.9°
0.05	87.1°
0.1	84.3°
0.2	78.7°
0.3	73.3°
0.4	68.2°
0.5	63.4°
0.6	59.0°
0.7	55.0°
0.8	51.3°
0.9	48.0°
1.0	45.0°
1.1	42.3°
1.2	39.8°

Table 11

APPENDIX C – BRIDGING DATA

Material	c	End supports	k
Mild steel	5.517	One fixed, other end loaded	1
Cast iron	3.625	One fixed, load distributed	1
Aluminium alloy	1.889	Both supported load in centre	4
English oak	1.182	Both supported load distributed	8
Red pine	1.025	Both fixed, load in centre	6
Fir (spruce)	0.946	Both fixed load distributed	12
Yellow pine	0.788		

Table 12

For rectangular section:
Minimum breaking force in kg $= \dfrac{breadth \times depth^2}{span} \times c \times k$,
where dimensions are in mm.

For round section: MBF (kg) $= \dfrac{diameter^3}{span} \times c \times k \times 0.589$.

To convert from solid to hollow rectangular multiply the MBF by a factor of $\dfrac{I_{(hollow)}}{I_{(solid)}}$, where $I_{(solid)} = \dfrac{bd^3}{12}$; from solid to angle multiply by a factor of $\dfrac{I_{angle}}{I_{solid}} \times \dfrac{d}{2 \times (d - c_x)}$. The values of the moment I and centroid distances are taken from the steel suppliers tables. Typical values are:

Dimension b×d×t (mm)	Vert centroid c_x (mm)	Section	Mass (kg/m)	I (mm⁴)
50x75x6	24.4	unequal angle	5.65	405,000
65x100x8	32.7	unequal angle	9.94	1,270,000
30x30x3.2	15.0	hollow rectangular	2.65	40,000
40x60x4	30.0	hollow rectangular	5.72	336,000
40x80x4	40.0	hollow rectangular	6.97	696,000
50x100x5	50.0	hollow rectangular	10.9	1,700,000
51x102	51.0	BS4:pt1 1980 channel	10.42	2,077,000
76x127	63.5	I Joist	16.37	5,694,000
50x75		solid		1,757,813
65x100		solid		5,416,667
30x30		solid		67,500
40x60		solid		720,000
40x80		solid		1,707,000
50x100		solid		4,166,667
51x102		solid		4,510,134
76x127		solid		12,973,092

Table 13

Supported ends, load in centre

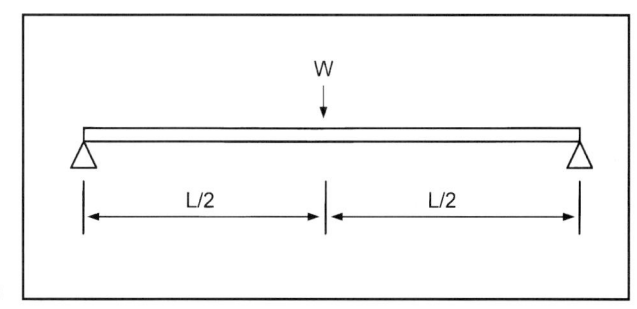

Figure 13

maximum deflection $= \dfrac{WL^3}{48EI}$

end slope $= \dfrac{WL^2}{16EI}$

57

Fixed ends, load in centre

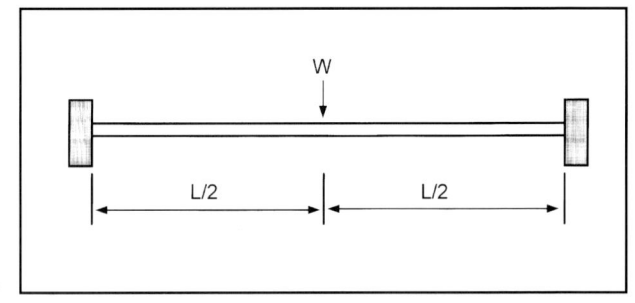

Figure 14

maximum deflection $= \dfrac{WL^3}{192EI}$

position of maximum deflection $= \dfrac{L}{2}$

Supported ends, load distributed

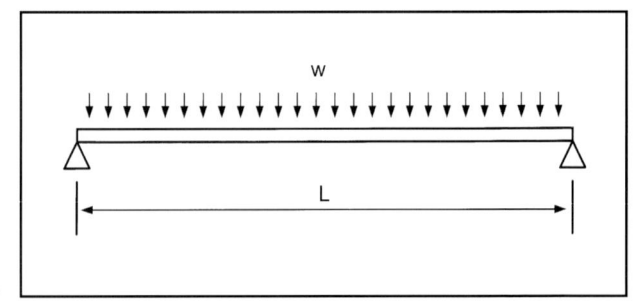

Figure 15

maximum deflection $= \dfrac{5wL^4}{384EI}$

end slope $= \dfrac{wL^3}{24EI}$, where w = load/unit length

Fixed ends, load distributed

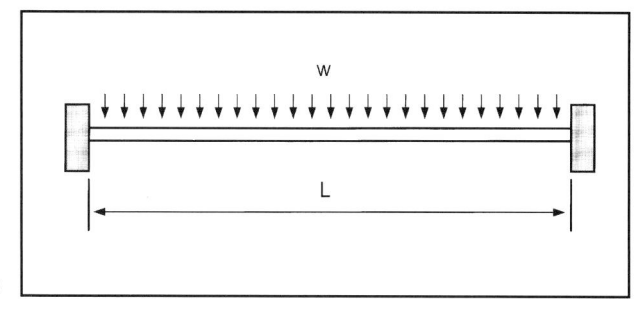

Figure 16

maximum deflection $= \dfrac{wL^4}{384EI}$

position of maximum deflection $= \dfrac{L}{2}$, where w = load/unit length

Moments of area

Solid rod
$$I = \dfrac{\pi D^4}{64}$$

Solid rectangle
$$I = \dfrac{BD^3}{12}$$

Round tube
$$I = \dfrac{\pi(D^4 - d^4)}{64}$$

Symmetrical hollow rectangular tube
$$I = \dfrac{BD^3 - bd^3}{12}$$

where: B is the outside width, D is the outside depth, or diameter,
b is the internal width, d is the internal depth or diameter.

Bending stress

$$\sigma = \frac{My}{I} = \frac{E}{R}$$

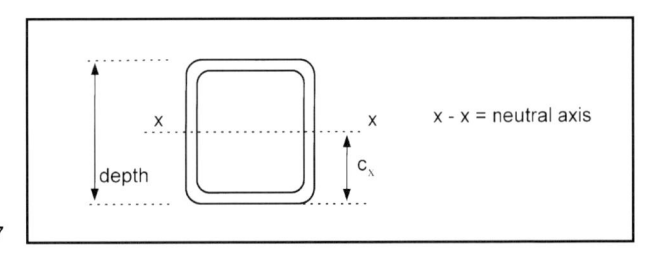

Figure 17

where;
σ = stress due to bending at a distance y from the neutral axis (N/m²),
M = bending moment (Nm), I = second moment of area (m⁴),
E = modulus of elasticity (Pa), R = radius of curvature (m),
y = depth − c_x.

Physical Properties

Material	Density ρ (kg/m³)	Modulus E (GPa)	Coeff of exp α (μm/mK)	Proof stress σ_y (MN/m²)	Yield stress σ_f (MN/m²)
Mild steel	7850	210	11	230–460	400–770
Stainless steels	8000	213	18	200–585	500–800
Cast iron	7150	110	11	–	100–300
Aluminium alloys	2720	70	23	30–280	90–300
Brass 65/35	8450	105	19	62–430	330–530
Copper	8960	104	11	47–320	200–350
Concrete	2400	14	–	–	27–55
Oak, with grain	~650	~12	~0.15	–	50–100
Spruce, with grain	~600	~14	~0.15	–	50–100
Spruce, across grain	~600	~0.5	~0.15	–	50–100

Table 14

Pascals (Pa) are a measure of pressure or stress in N/m². 1kgf = 9.807N where 1kgf is the force of a mass of 1kg under the influence of gravity (at 9.807m/s²). For practical purposes, kg are exchangeable with N after multiplying with the conversion factor. The lower values of σ_y and σ_f for steels refer to 'black' finish while the higher ones refer to heat-treated or high tensile material. The range of values for aluminium, copper and brass is due to the change in property caused by heat treatment and/or mechanical work.

APPENDIX D – ELECTRIC WINCH DATA

Typical ratings are as follows (courtesy of Superwinch):

Model	Drive	Winch capacity (lb)	Weight (kg)	No load speed (m/m)	Full load speed (m/m)	No load (A)	2000lb 908kg (A)	4000lb 1816kg (A)	6000lb 2724kg (A)	8500lb 3859kg (A)	9000lb 4086kg (A)	10000lb 4540kg (A)
X3	Planetary	4000	19	9.1	1.1	35	149	290				
X6	Planetary	6000	31	5.3	0.8	30	142	247	390			
Husky 8	Worm	8500	57	5.6	0.5	71	160	224	300	405		
X9	Planetary	9000	34	7.8	0.6	78	160	240	310		435	
Husky 10	Worm	10000	57	6.7	0.5	62	138	205	278			450

Table 15

This shows that it wouldn't take long to discharge a battery even with a minimal load! The winch performance is particularly dependant on the spool diameter and as layers are wound on, the effective torque and hence pull reduces. Use of a snatch block is recommended, but it will, of course, reduce the effective distance over which it is possible to winch.The weights shown are for a bare winch and do not include mounting plates, rope, fairleads, additional batteries and so on.

When fitted to a vehicle, the winch should have its own battery. That way, even if it becomes discharged the vehicle will not be disabled. This battery will need to be capable of very deep charge/discharge cycles. It should also be charged through a split-charging diode set. This isolates the winch and vehicle batteries while permitting charging to both. It is feasible to use battery cut-out switches instead, but it may well require additional heavy wiring around the engine compartment. The wiring is simpler and control automatic if diodes are used. If additional capacity is needed in an emergency, it is quite simple to use jump-start leads to parallel the batteries. A cut-out switch should always be fitted between the winch battery and control solenoids. If a solenoid becomes stuck or in other emergency, it is then a simple matter to disconnect power rapidly from the winch motor.

In theory, the maximum load likely to be imposed on a winch for self-recovery is around 1.2 times the vehicle deadweight. Fitting a winch with double the deadweight capacity will be sufficient for virtually all purposes. If the winch stalls in use, there is probably some other unseen obstruction, the only way to find out being to dig the ground away. When this has been done it will be a simple matter to use bridging ladders or logs to make the final task even easier.

APPENDIX E – CONVERSION FACTORS & FORMULAE

lb – kg	multiply by 0.454	litre – gallon (imp)	multiply by 0.220
ton – lb	multiply by 2240	gal – ft^3	multiply by 0.161
m – ft	multiply by 3.281	ft^2 – m^2	multiply by 0.093
in – mm	multiply by 25.4	in^3 – cm^3	multiply by 16.39
radian – degree	multiply by 57.296	m^3 – yd^3	multiply by 1.308
mile – km	multiply by 1.6103	hectare – acre	multiply by 2.471
lbf/in^2 – N/m^2	multiply by 6895	mph – metre/second	multiply by 0.4473
kgf/cm^2 – bar	multiply by 0.9807	Joules – kWH	multiply by 2.78×10^{-7}
kgf – N	multiply by 9.807	density of water (H$_2$O)	0.998kg/l
kgm – lbft	multiply by 7.227	density of sea water	1.025kg/l
lb/ft^2 – kg/m^2	multiply by 4.882	density of benzine	0.879kg/l
π	3.14159	acceleration due to gravity g	9.81ms^{-2}

Table 16

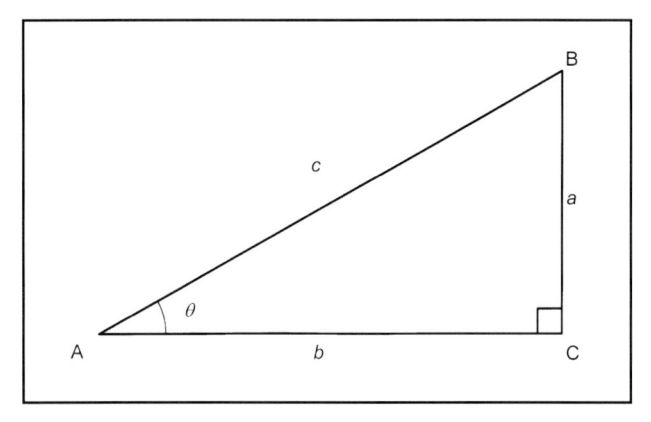

Figure 18a

$$\sin\theta = \frac{a}{c}, \quad a = c\sin\theta, \quad c = \frac{a}{\sin\theta}$$

$$\cos\theta = \frac{b}{c}, \quad b = c\cos\theta, \quad c = \frac{b}{\cos\theta}$$

$$\tan\theta = \frac{a}{b}, \quad a = b\tan\theta, \quad b = \frac{a}{\tan\theta}$$

$$\tan\theta = \frac{\sin\theta}{\cos\theta}$$

$$c^2 = a^2 + b^2$$

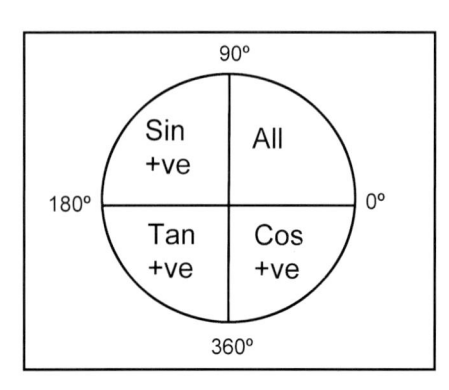

Quadrants where the trigonometric ratios have a positive value

Figure 18b

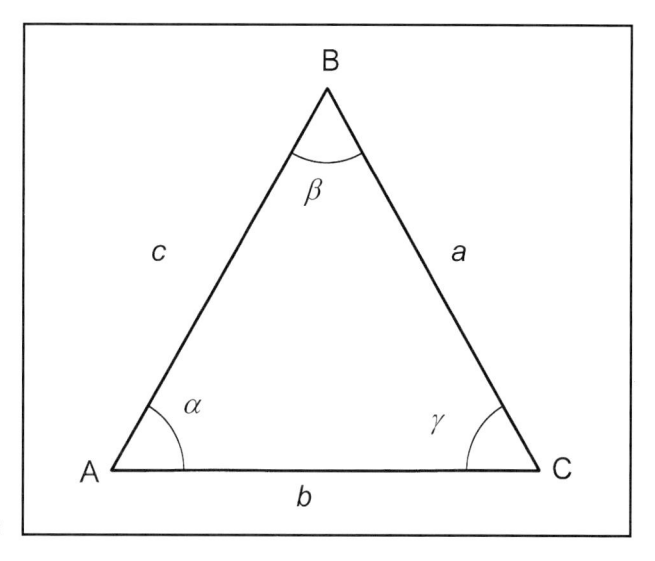

Figure 18c

$$\frac{a}{\sin\alpha} = \frac{b}{\sin\beta} = \frac{c}{\sin\gamma} = 2R$$

$a^2 = b^2 + c^2 - 2bc\cos\alpha$

$b^2 = a^2 + c^2 - 2ac\cos\beta$

$c^2 = a^2 + b^2 - 2ab\cos\gamma$

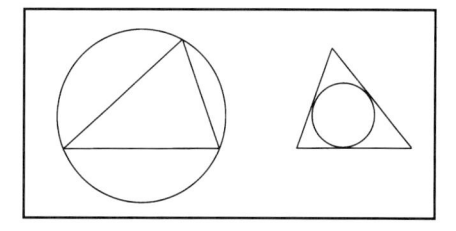

Figure 18d

Radius of the circumcircle, $R = \dfrac{abc}{4\Delta}$

Radius of inscribed circle, $r = \dfrac{\Delta}{s}$

where Δ = area of triangle = $\tfrac{1}{2}bc\sin\alpha$; and $s = \dfrac{a+b+c}{2}$

Kinetic energy = $\dfrac{m \times v^2}{2}$ Joules,

where m is the mass in kg and v the velocity in metres/second.

Degrees	Radians	Sin	Cos	Tan
0	0.0000	0.0000	1.0000	0.0000
5	0.0873	0.0872	0.9962	0.0875
10	0.1745	0.1736	0.9848	0.1763
15	0.2618	0.2588	0.9659	0.2679
20	0.3491	0.3420	0.9397	0.3640
25	0.4363	0.4226	0.9063	0.4663
30	0.5236	0.5000	0.8660	0.5774
35	0.6109	0.5736	0.8192	0.7002
40	0.6981	0.6428	0.7660	0.8391
45	0.7854	0.7071	0.7071	1.0000
50	0.8727	0.7660	0.6428	1.1918
55	0.9599	0.8192	0.5736	1.4281
60	1.0472	0.8660	0.5000	1.7321
65	1.1345	0.9063	0.4226	2.1445
70	1.2217	0.9397	0.3420	2.7475
75	1.3090	0.9659	0.2588	3.7321
80	1.3963	0.9848	0.1736	5.6713
85	1.4835	0.9962	0.0872	11.4301
90	1.5708	1.0000	0.0000	∞

Table 17

Number	Log
1.0	0.0000
1.5	0.1761
2.0	0.3010
2.5	0.3979
3.0	0.4771
3.5	0.5441
4.0	0.6021
4.5	0.6532
5.0	0.6990
5.5	0.7404
6.0	0.7782
6.5	0.8129
7.0	0.8451
7.5	0.8751
8.0	0.9031
8.5	0.9294
9.0	0.9542
9.5	0.9777
10	1.0000
100	2.0000
1,000	3.0000
10,000	4.0000
100,000	5.0000
1,000,000	6.0000

Table 18

Slope	Grade (%)	Angle (°)
1 in 20	5.0	2.9
1 in 18	5.6	3.2
1 in 16	6.3	3.6
1 in 14	7.1	4.1
1 in 12	8.3	4.8
1 in 10	10.0	5.7
1 in 9	11.1	6.3
1 in 8	12.5	7.1
1 in 7	14.3	8.1
1 in 6	16.7	9.5
1 in 5	20.0	11.3
1 in 4	25.0	14.0
1 in 3	33.3	18.4
1 in 2	50	26.6
1 in 1	100	45.0
1 in 0.5	200	63.4
1 in 0.25	400	76.0

Table 19

APPENDIX F – TYPICAL VEHICLE WEIGHTS & CAPACITIES

W/base (in)	W/base (mm)	Kerb weight (kg)	Max payload (kg)	GVW (kg)	Load per rear wheel (kg)	Working load (kg)
90	2286	1731	819	2550	842	900
100	2540	2080	660	2720	850	900
110	2794	1916	1200	3116	1079	1100

Table 20

The rear wheel loads are calculated on the assumption that the full load is evenly split across either side, all carried by the rear axle, and the basic weight split 50/50 front to rear. This is in excess of Maximum Axle Weight and therefore provides a small margin for changes in centre of gravity due to varying cambers, slopes and loads.

These figures are for typical Land Rover vehicles, in particular the Station Wagon variants, which are heavier than the utility versions. Most similar sized vehicles will be roughly the same weight, but in any event users should rely on the figures provided by the manufacturer of their own vehicles where appropriate.

REFERENCES

Kempe's Engineer's Year Book.

Engineer Field Data; US Army.

Strength of Materials; Arnold.

Structural Mechanics; Durka, Morgan and Williams.

Mechanical Engineer's Data Handbook; Carvill.

Engineering Mathematics; Stroud.

Registered Trademarks

Jackall	Jackall Europe Ltd, Bridgend
Superwinch	Superwinch Ltd, Tavistock
Tirfor	Tirfor Ltd, Sheffield
Land Rover	Land Rover Ltd, Solihull

Photographic Credits

Cover illustrations
Front & Rear: *Land Rover World*

Text illustrations
Nick Cole: 2, 13, 15, 18, 21, 22, 25, 31, 33, 34, 37, 40, 48, 49.
Roger Lancaster: 10, 72.
Land Rover World: 6, 8, 26, 50.
Off Road & 4 Wheel Drive: 23, 44, 45, 46.

Boldly go…